AI EXPLORER

LEVEL - 1

BY - A. K. SAI

BLUEROSE PUBLISHERS
India | U.K.

For permissions requests or inquiries regarding this publication,
please contact:

BLUEROSE PUBLISHERS
www.BlueRoseONE.com
info@bluerosepublishers.com
+91 8882 898 898
+4407342408967

ISBN: 978-93-7542-334-8

First Edition: February 2026

Acknowledgements

I offer my heartfelt gratitude to **Bhagawan Sri Sathya Sai Baba**, my spiritual guide, whose teachings and values have been a constant source of inspiration and guidance in my life.

I would like to sincerely thank my brother, **Gorthipalli Dhiraj Kumar**, an English teacher by profession, for carefully proofreading this book and helping improve its language, clarity, and readability.

I am deeply grateful to my parents for their constant encouragement, patience, and belief in this work. Their support has been a strong source of motivation throughout this journey.

This book was shaped with the intention of helping young learners understand Artificial Intelligence in a simple, responsible, and meaningful way. As AI becomes an important part of everyday life, children too deserve the opportunity to learn about it thoughtfully and safely.

I also acknowledge the support provided by **BlueRose Publishers** in assisting with the publication of this book. I am thankful to everyone who supported this effort, directly or indirectly.

PREFACE — AI EXPLORER LEVEL 1

Artificial Intelligence is already part of our everyday lives — from the videos we watch to the maps we use to travel.
Yet for many children, **AI feels confusing, mysterious, or even scary**.
This book was created to change that.

AI Explorer – Level 1 introduces young learners to the world of AI in a simple, friendly, and engaging way.
It does not teach coding.
Instead, it focuses on helping children understand:

- what AI is
- what AI is not
- how AI learns
- and how AI should be used responsibly

Through stories, activities, and familiar examples, this book encourages curiosity, critical thinking, and safe digital habits.

Our goal is not to make children experts in AI — but to help them become **confident and thoughtful users of AI**.

This book is the first step in a learning journey that will grow with the child in future levels.

NOTE FOR PARENTS & TEACHERS

This book is designed to give children around ages 10–12 a beginner friendly first look at Artificial Intelligence (AI).

It is not a coding book. Instead, it builds:

- AI literacy – what AI is and is not
- Simple ideas of machine learning and deep learning
- Awareness of safety, privacy, and fairness
- Good habits for using AI as a helper, not a boss

How you can use this book:

- Read and discuss the pages together.
- Let the child color, circle, and write in their own words.
- Use the stories to talk about real apps your family uses (maps, videos, music, etc.).
- When pages ask "Who should decide?" or "Is this fair?", treat them as conversation starters, not tests.

Key messages for children:

- AI can be very helpful, but it can also make mistakes.
- AI should be used as a tool, not as the final judge.
- Personal information (full name, address, phone, passwords) should never be shared with AI.
- If an answer feels mean, scary, or wrong, children should stop and ask an adult.

We hope this book helps your child become a curious, careful, and kind AI user.

TABLE OF CONTENTS

ME & THE AI SQUAD

Smart helpers that will travel with you in this book.

DATA ROBOT
Loves numbers
and
examples

PATTERN DRAGON
Spots patterns
and
rules

???
A secret AI helper
will join later...

"What is the book about?"

In this book, you will learn what AI (Artificial Intelligence) is and how smart helpers like these can learn from data, spot patterns, and sometimes even make mistakes.

Activity

1. Color DATA ROBOT and PATTERN DRAGON.
2. Look at the mystery circle (???).
   Write a name for this secret AI helper:
   My name for this helper: ______________________

GUESS THE SECRET HELPER

In the previous page, you met DATA ROBOT and PATTERN DRAGON, and a secret third helper (???).
Now let's think about what this helper might do.

Activity block

1. What might this helper be good at?
   "This helper will be good at
   ____."

2. Tick all the jobs that match your idea
   □ Keeping things fair
   □ Keeping things safe
   □ Finding mistakes
   □ Helping people feel okay
   □ Something else: ________________________

3. What should an AI helper never do?
   "An AI helper should never
   ____."

4. Draw a small symbol that matches your idea for this helper.
   (Hints: lightbulb, lock, heart, scale ...)

CHAPTER 1 – WHAT IS AI?

What is AI?
AI = Artificial Intelligence

AI is when a computer or machine does a job in a smart way – by learning from data, spotting patterns, or making choices, instead of just following a very simple fixed rule.

In this book, we will see AI helpers that:

- look at lots of data (like DATA ROBOT),
- find patterns and rules (like PATTERN DRAGON), and
- sometimes even make mistakes that we must check.

Video app recommends videos

Phone unlocks with your face

Email catches spam messages

Quick Check

1. Underline the words in the box above that explain what AI does.
(Hint: "learning from data", "spotting patterns", "making choices".)

2. Put a ✓ under each picture that shows AI helping.
(All three should get a ✓.)

3. In your own words, finish this sentence:
"To me, AI is when a computer ______________________________."

ACTIVITY – WHERE IS THE AI?

Use what you learned about AI to spot where it is helping

 Video app suggesting videos	 Fan with on/off switch	 Phone unlocking with your face	 Story book
 Email catching spam	 Traffic light with fixed timer	 App suggesting what to study next	 Football

1. For each picture, decide if it uses AI.
 Put a ✓ in the corner of the box if you think it uses AI.
 Put an ✗ in the corner if you think it does not use AI.
2. Count your checks.
 How many AI examples are on this page?
 Number of ✓ : ________
3. Write two places where YOU use AI the most in your life.
 a) ______________________________________
 b) ______________________________________
4. Choose ONE picture from the grid.
 Explain in one sentence how AI is helping there.
"In the __________ picture, AI helps by ____________________________
____."

HOW AI SEES PATTERNS

AI is very good at spotting patterns.
A pattern is something that repeats in a rule.

For example:

- 2, 4, 6, 8, 10... (adding 2 each time)
- △ △ ○, △ △ ○ , △ △ .... (two triangles, then a circle)

Pattern Dragon loves finding these rules in data.

□	□	□
○	○	○
★	★	?

Number pattern: 2 4 6 8 __

What should go in the last box?

Quick Pattern Tasks

1. Fill in the missing shape and number.
   - Draw the missing shape in the empty box of the grid.
   - Write the missing number: 2, 4, 6, 8, __
2. Color the patterns.
   - Color each row of shapes in a different color.
3. Explain the rule in one sentence.

"The rule in the number pattern is:

____."

(Hint: How much are we adding each time?)

MORE PATTERN FUN

Pattern Dragon has a few quick puzzles for you.

△△○△△○ [ ]

1. Shape pattern

a) Look at the pattern of triangles and circles.
Draw the shape that should go in the last box.

b) What is the rule in this pattern?
"Two ________________, then one ________________, repeat."

5 10 15 20 [ ]

2. Number pattern

a) Write the missing number in the last box:
5, 10, 15, 20, ____

b) How much are we adding each time?
"We add _________ each time."

3. Make your own pattern

In the boxes below, draw or write your own pattern.
You can use shapes, symbols, or small numbers.

[ ][ ][ ][ ][ ][ ]

Now explain the rule in one sentence:
"My pattern rule is:
______________________________________."

Checking Time: Ask a friend if they can guess your pattern rule.

HOW AI LEARNS FROM EXAMPLES

AI does not start out knowing everything.
We have to train it using many examples and the right answer.
DATA ROBOT looks at the examples and learns:
"This is a fruit." "This is not a fruit."
Later, it can guess for new things it has not seen before.

	Yes/No

TRAINING TIME – Quick Tasks

1. Color the answers.
 Give each "Yes" box a single color, and each "No" box a different color.
2. Add your own example.
 In the last row, write the name of one thing.
 Decide if it is a fruit and circle Yes or No.
3. What did the AI learn?
 In your own words, complete this sentence:

"From this table, our AI learns that a fruit is usually ______________________________________." *(eatable/ not eatable)*

ACTIVITY – TRAIN YOUR MINI-AI

Use examples to teach your own simple AI.

Fruit or Not?

Thing	Is this Fruit?	My label for AI
Apple	YES / NO	
Ball	YES / NO	
Grape	YES / NO	
Chair	YES / NO	
Orange	YES / NO	
Pencil	YES / NO	

1. Fruit training table.

For each thing, decide if it is a fruit.

a) In column 2, circle Yes or No.

b) In column 3, write the same answer(*Yes/No*) for your AI.

(You are giving labels to train your mini-AI.)

2. What if you teach it wrong?

Imagine you circle "Yes" for Ball by mistake.

a) Later, your AI sees a ball.

What will it say?

"This is a ________________."

b) Why is it important to give correct examples to AI?

"It is important because

____

_____."

(Pet or Not?)

Thing	Is it a pet?
Dog	YES / NO
Tiger	YES / NO
Fish in the Bowl	YES / NO
Rock	YES / NO
?	YES / NO

3. Train a different AI

This time, you are training an AI to tell if something is a pet.

For each thing in the table:

a) Circle Yes if it could be kept as a pet, or No if not.

b) If you want, add one more row with your own example.

WHEN AI GETS IT WRONG

AI is not perfect.
Sometimes it sees patterns that are wrong or gets confused.
That's why we need a helper who checks the AI's answers and asks, "Is this right and fair?"

Wise Owl

Panel 1 – AI's wrong guess

Panel 2 – Wise Owl checks and corrects

Quick Thinking

1. What mistake did the AI make in Panel 1?
"It called a __________ ."
2. Why is Wise Owl important? "Wise Owl helps by _______________ _____________________________."
3. Where in your life should you not trust AI blindly?
(Tick all you think are important.)
☐ Choosing which exam answers are correct
☐ Deciding if a person is good or bad
☐ Suggesting fun videos to watch
☐ Helping you check spelling in homework

WISE OWL'S CHECK-UP

Help Wise Owl decide when we should trust AI and when we should check carefully.

1. Exam Email in Spam

Riya's exam details were sent by her teacher. The email app's AI moved it to the Spam folder by mistake.

Is the AI doing a good job here? Circle one: OK / Not OK

What should Riya do?

"Riya should ___________________________________."

Hint: Where do we look if something important is missing?

2. Wrong Person in a Photo

An AI on a photo app says, "Is this your mother?" but the picture is actually of your friend from school.

Is the AI doing a good job here? Circle one: OK / Not OK

What should you do?

"I should _______________________________________."

Hint: Do you accept wrong tags, or fix them?

3. Video Suggestions

A video app's AI suggests a funny cartoon video. You like it and it is okay for your age.

Is the AI doing a good job here? Circle one: OK / Not OK

What should you still remember?

"I should remember that ____________________________."

Hint: Who decides what you finally watch – you or the AI?

WISE OWL'S QUESTIONS

4. Tick the things where you should be extra careful with AI:

□ Checking exam answers

□ Choosing if a person is good or bad

□ Picking a fun cartoon to watch

□ Unlocking your phone

5. In your own words: "We should not always trust AI because ____."

AI EXPLORER – LEVEL 1 CHECKPOINT

Before you move on, let's see what you remember about AI.

Task 1 – What is AI?

1. Which one best explains AI?
Circle the best answer.
a) A computer that only follows one simple rule
b) A computer that can learn from data and spot patterns
c) A machine that is big, loud and made of metal

Task 2 – AI or Not? (quick)

2. Tick the things that usually use AI:
□ A video app recommending new videos
□ A simple hand fan
□ A phone unlocking with your face
□ A story book
□ An email app catching spam

Task 3 – Pattern + Data

3. Fill in the blanks:
a) In the pattern 2, 4, 6, 8, ____,
we keep adding ______ each time.
b) When we show AI many examples with the right answers,
we call that training with __________.

You finished Chapter 1 –
Great job, AI Explorer!

Signed by: ______________________
(Parent / Guardian / Teacher)

This badge belongs to:

MY AI THOUGHTS

Think about everything you learnt in chapter 1 and write your ideas here.

1. What I learnt about AI

- One thing I learnt is:

Hint: Think of something we did in this chapter – like patterns, data, or AI making mistakes.

- Another thing I learnt is:

Hint: You can write about DATA ROBOT, PATTERN DRAGON, or WISE OWL and what they do.

- One example of AI, I did not notice before is:

Hint: Think of apps that suggest something – videos, routes, songs, or study topics.

2. How I feel about AI

- AI makes me feel (curious / excited / worried / something else):

Hint: Look back at all the pages. Did you feel more excited, curious, or sometimes a bit worried?

- I think AI is helpful when:

Hint: Think of times when AI saves time or makes something easier for you.

- I think we should be careful with AI when:

Hint: Remember the pages where AI was wrong or where WISE OWL asked us to check the answer.

My idea for a new AI helper

Name of my AI helper:

What it helps me with:

Draw your AI helper

Hint: You can mix a job and an animal, like "Homework Hawk" or "Pattern Panda".
Hint: What problem would you like this helper to solve in your daily life – homework, focus, practice, fun, or safety?

CHAPTER 2 – HOW AI MAKES DECISIONS

YES OR NO?
HOW AI ASKS QUESTIONS???

AI often makes decisions by asking yes or no questions.
Example:
"Is it an animal?"
If yes, go one way.
If no, go another way.

Many yes/no questions together can help AI choose the right answer.

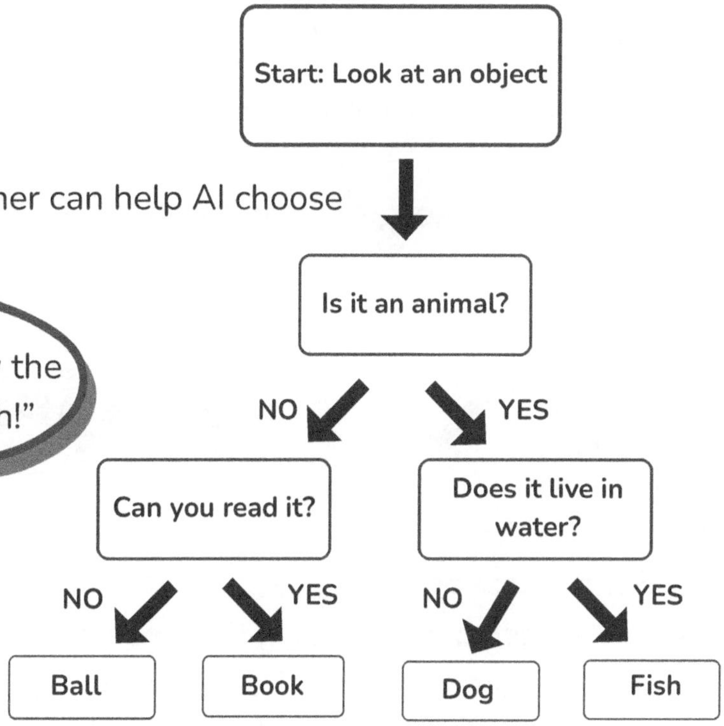

Pattern Dragon

TRY THE YES/NO PATHS

1. Trace the paths.

a) Start at the top and follow the YES/NO arrows to reach Fish.
Draw over the correct path with your pencil.

b) Now start again and follow the arrows to reach Book.
Trace that path with a different style (dotted line if you like).

2. Answer these questions:

a) Which question decides between Fish and Dog?
"Does it ________________________________?"

b) Which question decides between Book and Ball?
"Can you ________________________________?"

3. In your own words:
"A yes/no question is a question where the only answers are
__________________________."

ACTIVITY – FOLLOW THE YES/NO PATH

Use the yes/no questions to put each object in the right place.

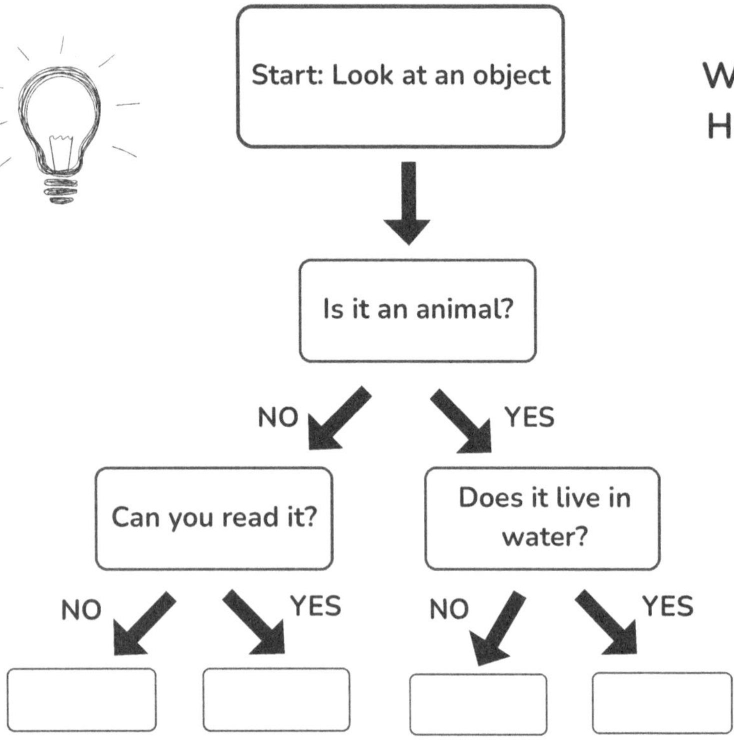

Word bank (use each once):
Horse, Fish, Novel, Football

1. Fill the leaves.

Use the yes/no questions in the tree and write each word from the word bank into the correct leaf box.
(Hint: Only animals go on the YES side of Q1.)

2. Trace two paths.

a) Start at the top and follow the arrows to Fish.
Trace that path with your pencil.
b) Start again and follow the arrows to Novel.
Trace that path with a dotted line if you like.

3. Your own yes/no question.

Imagine you want to separate "things you can eat" from "things you cannot eat."
Write a yes/no question you could ask:
"____ ?"
(Hint: Start with "Can you eat it...?" or something similar.)

AI'S QUESTION GAME

Sometimes AI guesses things by asking many yes/no questions, just like a "What am I?" game.

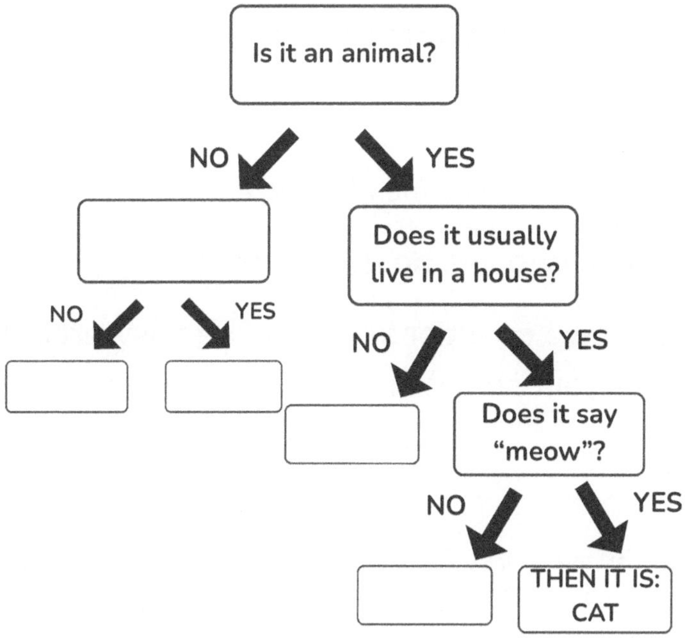

TRY THE QUESTION GAME

1. Answer for "cat".

Pretend the secret object is a cat.

For each question, circle YES or NO.

Q1: Is it an animal? → YES / NO

Q2: Does it usually live in a house? → YES / NO

Q3: Does it say "meow"? → YES / NO

2. Think of a different animal.

Choose one animal (not a cat):

My animal: ____________________

Now answer the same questions for your animal:

Q1: Is it an animal? → YES / NO

Q2: Does it usually live in a house? → YES / NO

Q3: Does it say "meow"? → YES / NO

3. What did you notice?

"This AI question game is good for guessing __________,

but it cannot guess __________."

MAKE YOUR OWN QUESTION GAME

Use yes/no questions to help an AI guess your secret object.

1. Choose a secret object

Pick one object from this list, or think of your own:
Word list: dog, bus, apple, book, chair, fish
My secret object is:
Hint: Don't tell your friend or the AI yet!

2. Write two yes/no questions

Write two questions that can be answered with yes or no and help the AI guess your secret object.
Q1: ____ ?
Q2: ____ ?

Hint: You can start with things like "Is it an animal?", "Can you eat it?", "Is it used in school?", "Can it move on its own?"

3. Test your AI question game

Imagine someone is trying to guess your secret object. They will answer only YES or NO to your questions.
a) If the answer to both questions is YES, your object might be:
b) If the answer to one or both questions is NO, what other object from the word list could it be?
Hint: Check if your questions help separate your object from the others in the list.

4. Share your game

Show your yes/no questions to a friend, parent, or teacher.
Ask them to guess your secret object by answering YES or NO only.
Were your questions helpful?
"My question game worked / did not work because
____."

- Use this space for rough work

IF THIS... THEN THAT!

AI can use yes/no questions to make rules.
A rule tells it:
"If this is true... then do that."
Pattern Dragon loves turning questions into rules.

RULE BOARD

1.If it is an animal and lives in water, then it is a fish.
2.If it is an animal and lives on land, then it is a dog.
3.If it is not an animal and you can read it, then it is a book.

Pattern Dragon

TRY USING RULES

1. Fill in the missing word.

a) If it is an animal and lives in water, then it is a ________.

b) If it is not an animal and you can read it, then it is a ________.

2. Turn a question into a rule.

Question: "Is it an animal?"

Write a rule using If... then...

"If it is not an animal, then ____."

(Hint: Think of things that are not animals.)

RULE MATCHING GAME

Match each rule to the objects it fits.

Rule A	Rule B	Rule C
If it is an animal and lives in water, then it goes in Box A.	If it is an animal and lives on land, then it goes in Box B.	If it is not an animal and you can read it, then it goes in Box C.

Tasks

1. Match objects to rules.

For each object, write A, B, or C under it to show which rule box it belongs to.
(If it does not fit any rule, write X.)

2. Think and check:

a) Which objects go with Rule A?
Answer: ____________________________

b) Which objects go with Rule B?
Answer: ____________________________

c) Which objects go with Rule C?
Answer: ____________________________

3. Your own small rule.

Write one new rule using If... then...

"If it ______________________________________,
then it ______________________________________."

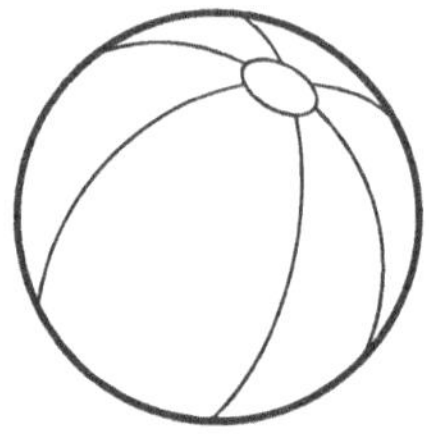

Ball

[ ]

Notebook

[ ]

Dog

[ ]

Fish

[ ]

Book

[ ]

Bird

[ ]

AI DECIDES OR I DECIDE?

For each situation, tick who should decide most of the time.

1. What video to watch next	□ AI	□ ME / ADULT
2. Whether an exam answer is correct	□ AI	□ ME / ADULT
3. Who should be punished at school	□ AI	□ ME / ADULT
4. How to spell a difficult word	□ AI	□ ME / ADULT

2. In your own words:

a) One thing I am happy to let AI help with:

b) One thing I think humans should always decide:

c) One good question to ask before trusting an AI decision:

"____ ?"

Scratch Pad

DECISION MASTER – CHECKPOINT

Let's see what you remember about yes/no questions and rules.

Quick recap questions

1. Which of these is a good yes/no question?

Circle ONE.

a) What is your favourite fruit?

b) Is this a fruit?

c) Why do you like fruit?

2. Fill in the missing word.

"If it is an animal and lives in water, then it is probably a __________."

3. When should AI ask more questions, before deciding?

Tick all that make sense.

□ Choosing which cartoon to show next

□ Deciding which medicine a person must take

□ Sorting photos into "cat" and "not cat"

□ Choosing who should get punished at school

YES / NO

?

You finished Chapter 2 –
Great job, AI Explorer!

Signed by: ____________________

(Parent / Guardian / Teacher)

This badge belongs to:

CHAPTER 3 – MACHINES THAT LEARN

WHAT IS MACHINE LEARNING?

Machine learning is when a computer learns from data and examples instead of just following fixed rules.

QUICK THINKING

1. Fill in the blank:
"Machine learning is when a computer learns from
______________________________."
(Hint: Look at the definition box.)

2. Tick the better sentence:
Machine learning means:
☐ The computer only follows one rule forever.
☐ The computer gets better by seeing many examples.

Step 1 - Training

 → "fruit"

 → "not fruit"

 → "fruit"

We show Data Robot many examples and the right answers.

Step 2 - Learning

Data Robot looks at all the examples and learns a pattern:
"Fruits are things we can eat that grow on plants or trees."

Step 3 - New Object

Later, we show a new picture:
Data Robot guesses: "This is a fruit."

IS THIS MACHINE LEARNING?

Tick "**ML**" if the computer learns from examples.
Tick "**Not ML**" if it just follows fixed rules.

A. Calculator You type **123 + 456**. It gives the answer. □ ML □ Not ML	**B. Music app** You listen to many **songs**. It starts **suggesting** new songs you might like. □ ML □ Not ML
C. Traffic light timer The light stays green for 30 seconds, then red for 30 seconds, again and again. □ ML □ Not ML	**D. Email spam filter** At first it misses some spam emails. When you mark “This is spam”, later it catches **similar** mails better. □ ML □ Not ML

THINK ABOUT IT

1. What does machine learning need?
Tick all that you think are important:
□ Many examples
□ Only one simple rule
□ Correct answers (labels)
□ Magic

2. In your own words:
“One place in my life where I think machine learning is used is:
______________________________________.”

TRAINING TIME VS QUIZ TIME

Machine Learning has study time and quiz time.

TRAINING TIME (STUDY)

Data Robot sees many examples
with the right answers.
This is called training.

QUIZ TIME (TEST)

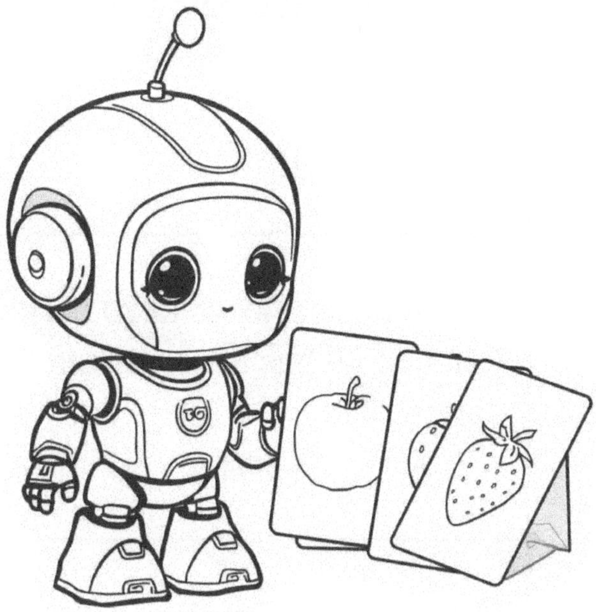

Now Data Robot sees new pictures
without the answers.
This is called testing.

QUICK CHECK

1. In training time, does Data Robot see the correct answers?
Circle: YES / NO

2. In quiz time, does Data Robot see the correct answers first?
Circle: YES / NO

3. Fill in the blanks:
"Training is like ____________ time.
Testing is like ____________ time."
(Hint: Think of when you study and when you write an exam.)

TRAINING OR TESTING?

For each picture, decide if Data Robot is in training or testing.

A. Data Robot sees a picture of an apple with the word “**fruit**” under it. □ Training □ Testing	**B.** Data Robot sees a picture of a ball with **no answer** written. □ Training □ Testing
C. Data Robot looks at **20 cards**. Every card has a picture and the correct label. □ Training □ Testing	D. Data Robot is trying to guess and we **check how many answers** are right. □ Training □ Testing
E. Data Robot makes a mistake. A human shows the **right answer** and fixes it. □ Training □ Testing	F. Data Robot sees a **new fruit picture** it has never seen before and has to guess. □ Training □ Testing

THINK ABOUT IT

1. Why do we need testing?
“Testing tells us
if the model is ______________________________.’

2. Tick one:
Machine learning models should be:
□ Only good at training questions
□ Good at new questions too

DATA, LABELS & DATASETS

Machine learning needs lots of data with the right labels.

Data = the examples we give to the computer.
Label = the correct answer for each example.
Dataset = a big table of examples and labels.

Data Robot collects data –
Names(examples) of many things.

THING	LABEL
Dog	Pet
Cat	Pet
Rock	Not Pet
Chair	Not Pet

This is a **dataset**:
a table of data (**things**)
and labels (**answers**).

1. Circle the word that means “the correct answer”:

Data   **L**abel   **D**ataset

2. Fill in the blanks:

a) The things we collect (like dog, cat, rock) are called ____________.

b) The words like “pet” or “not pet” are the ____________.

c) A big table of examples and labels is called a ____________.

FIX THE DATASET!

Some labels in this dataset are wrong. Help Data Robot fix them.

Data Robot

THING	LABEL	CORRECT(YES/ NO)
Dog	Pet	YES / NO
Tiger	Pet	YES / NO
Rock	Pet	YES / NO
Chair	Not Pet	YES / NO
Golfish	Not Pet	YES / NO
Car	Not Pet	YES / NO

1. Check each label.

For each Thing, look at the Label.
In the last column, circle:
Yes if the label is correct,
No if the label is wrong.

2. Fix the wrong ones.

Rewrite the correct labels:

a) Tiger → ____________________________
b) Rock → ____________________________
c) Goldfish → _________________________

3. Why are correct labels important?

"If the labels are wrong, the model will ____."

Hint: Think: Which of these can really be kept as a pet at home?

"Wrong labels → wrong learning!"

WHAT IS A MODEL?

After training, the computer has a “model” that can make guesses.

When we train a machine learning system with lots of data and labels, it creates a model.

A model is like the computer’s “trained brain” that makes predictions.

Using the trained model
(The model was already trained in the previous page.)

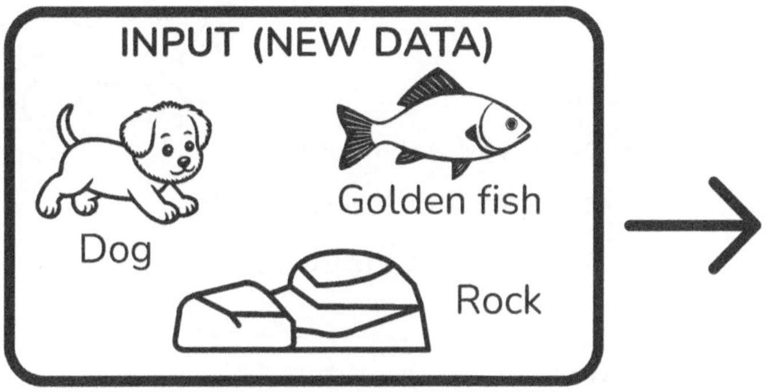

CHECK YOUR UNDERSTANDING

1. Fill in the blanks:
“A model is the computer’s trained ________ that makes ________.”

2. Tick the better sentence:
A model is:
□ Just a picture of a robot
□ The part of AI that makes guesses after training

3. Who helped the model learn patterns? (Tick one)
□ Data Robot
□ Pattern Dragon
□ Wise Owl

(Hint: Look at the drawing!)

Does the MODEL GUESS GOOD?

Wise Owl checks if the model's predictions are correct.

Data Robot Says
Dog → Pet

Dog
Model says: pet
Is this correct? □ Yes □ No
If not, correct label: _______________

Tiger
Model says: pet
Is this correct? □ Yes □ No
If not, correct label: _______________

Rock
Model says: not pet
Is this correct? □ Yes □ No
If not, correct label: _______________

Goldfish
Model says: not pet
Is this correct? □ Yes □ No
If not, correct label: _______________

Cat
Model says: pet
Is this correct? □ Yes □ No
If not, correct label: _______________

WISE OWL'S QUESTIONS

1. Which guesses were wrong?
"The model was wrong for:
_____________________________________."

2. Why is it important to check the model?
"It is important because
_____________________________________."

3. Tick one:
□ Models are always perfect.
□ Models can make mistakes,
so humans must check and fix them.

BUILD A TINY SCHOOL HELPER AI

Data Robot and Pattern Dragon want to train an AI to **spot** school things.

Data Robot wants to help **sort** school things.
Pattern Dragon loves patterns like “used at school” or “used for play”.
We will give the AI examples with labels like:
“pencil → school stuff”, “toy car → not school stuff”.

YOUR TURN

1. Bucket the 'school stuff' and 'not school stuff'.
Write the names of two school things:

Write the names of two not-school things:

2. Imagine we are making a dataset.
Tick which objects should go in “SCHOOL STUFF”:
☐ Pencil ☐ Toy car ☐ Notebook
☐ Apple ☐ Football ☐ Eraser

MAKE YOUR OWN MINI DATASET

Create some training data for your school helper AI.

1. Training data (study time)

THING	Label (School/Not School)	My drawing (optional)
Pencil		
Notebook		
Toy Car		
Apple		
___________		

For each Thing:

a) In the Label column, write "School" or "Not school".

b) In the last column, you can draw a tiny picture of it (or leave it blank if you don't want to draw).

2. Test data (quiz time)

Now think of two more objects to test your AI. Do not write the label yet.

Test example 1: ___________________________

Test example 2: ___________________________

(Later, you or an adult can ask: "Would our model say School or Not school?")

3. Explain like an AI builder

Fill in the blanks:

"I gave my AI training data with examples like ______________________________.
Then I made test data with new things like ______________________________.
My AI should learn to tell school stuff from not school stuff."

Wise Owl says:

"Good datasets are the first step to good models!"

GUESS THE RULE LIKE A MODEL

Pattern Dragon sees examples and tries to find the hidden rule.

Set 1 (numbers):	Set 2 (words):
2 → 4	DOG → animal
3 → 6	CAT → animal
4 → 8	CAR → not animal

CAN YOU FIND THE RULE?

1. For Set 1:

2 → 4, 3 → 6, 4 → 8

a) What rule could give these answers?

"Maybe the rule is: multiply by ______."

b) If the input is 5, what will the output be?

5 → ______

2. For Set 2:

DOG → animal

CAT → animal

CAR → not animal

a) What is the model looking at?

"It checks if something is an ____________."

b) Write one more example that fits this rule:

________ → animal

________ → not animal

3. Tick one:

□ A model always tells the rule in words.

□ Sometimes we only see input and output, and we have to guess the rule.

RULE PUZZLES FOR MINI MODELS

Pretend you are the model. Use the examples to guess the rule.

PUZZLE 1 – NUMBERS

The model sees these examples:

1 → 3

2 → 5

3 → 7

a) What could the rule be?

"Start with the number, then add ______."

b) Use your rule:

4 → ______

5 → ______

PUZZLE 3 – WORDS

The model sees these examples:

MATH → subject

SCIENCE → subject

PIZZA → not subject

a) What is the rule?

"If the word is a ____________, the model says subject."

b) Write one more word for each:

________ → subject

________ → not subject

PUZZLE 2 – SHAPES

The model sees these examples:

△ → "sharp"

□ → "sharp"

◯ → "not sharp"

a) What is the model looking at?

"It checks if the shape has ____________."

b) Look at this new shape: ★ (a star shape you draw).

Would the model say "sharp" or "not sharp"?

□ sharp □ not sharp

WISE OWL ASKS:

"Sometimes we can guess the rule from examples, just like a model does. But we also need to check if the rule is fair and makes sense."

DEEP LEARNING: MANY TINY HELPERS

Deep learning uses many tiny helpers in layers to spot patterns.

Deep learning is a kind of **machine learning** that uses many **tiny helpers** in **layers** to find complex patterns (like in pictures or sounds).

Many helpers working together = **a neural network.**

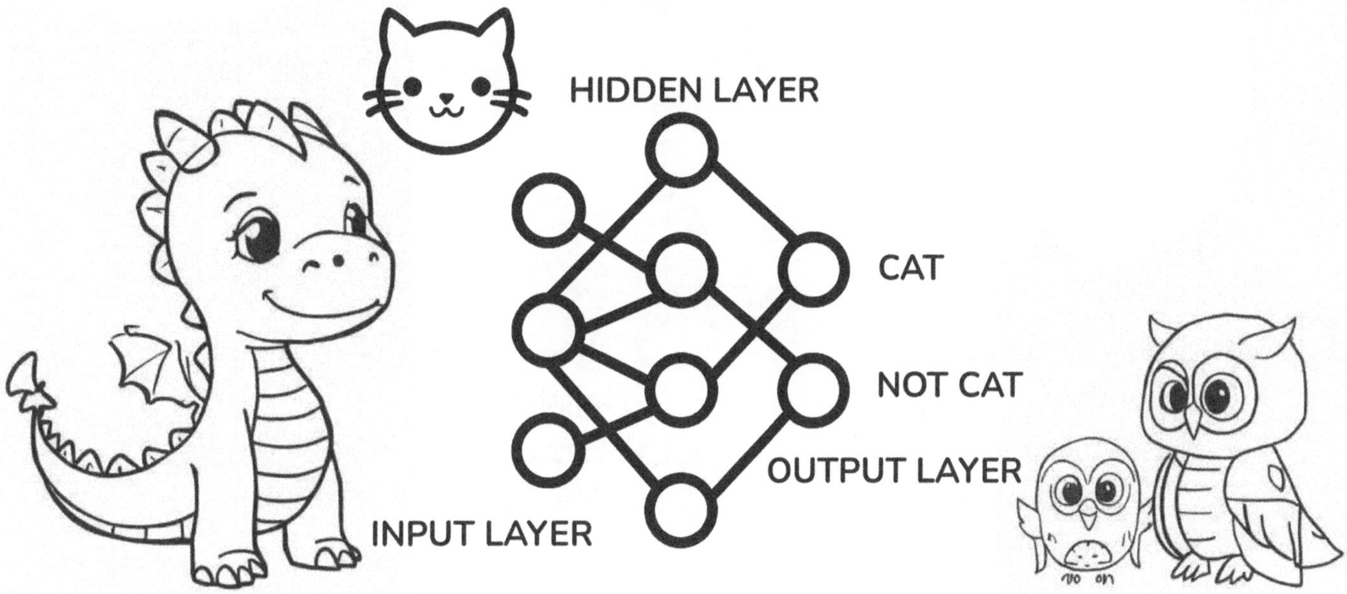

The **input layer** sees simple things like "whiskers?", "pointy ears?", "four legs?".
The **hidden layer** mixes these pieces to see bigger shapes like "cat face".
The **output layer** gives a prediction: Cat or Not Cat.

QUICK CHECK

1. Tick the name for this kind of layered system:

- □ robot costume
- □ neural network
- □ traffic light

2. Fill in the blanks:

Deep learning uses many tiny helpers in ____________, not just one rule.

3. Color suggestion (optional):

- Color the input layer dots one color.
- Color the hidden layer dots a second color.
- Color the output layer dots a third color.

FOLLOW THE PATH THROUGH THE LAYERS

Pretend you are a signal moving through a neural network.

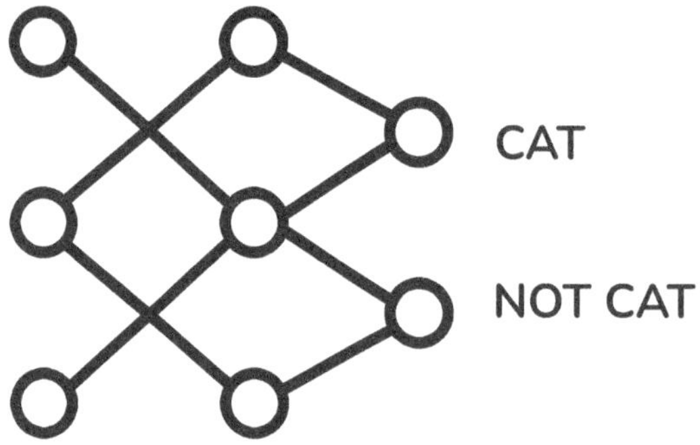

Instructions

1. Choose a "cat signal".

Imagine the input says:

- "Has whiskers" → YES
- "Has pointy ears" → YES
- "Has four legs" → YES

Start at the input dots and draw a path through the middle dots to the CAT output.

2. Now try a "not cat" signal.

Imagine the input says:

- "Has wheels" → YES
- "Has whiskers" → NO
- "Has four legs" → NO

Start again at the input dots and draw a path to the NOT CAT output.
(You can use a different style of line (e.g., dotted) for the second path.)

THINK ABOUT THE HELPERS

1. Do all helpers do everything, or does each dot do a small job?

□ One helper does everything alone

□ Many helpers each do a small job

2. Fill in the blank:

"Deep learning is good at spotting ____________ patterns, like in pictures."

3. Wise Owl says:

"Even deep models can make mistakes.
Should humans still check important decisions?"

□ Yes □ No

HOW DEEP LEARNING SEES PICTURES

Instead of looking at the whole picture at once,
it looks at small pieces and finds patterns.

Deep learning can chop a picture into squares.
It looks at each square to find small patterns like edges, corners, whiskers, and ears.
Then it combines these small patterns to decide:
"Is this a cat or not a cat?"

TRY IT YOURSELF

1. Which squares matter?

Look at the cat picture with the grid.
Lightly shade or circle the squares that have:

- Ears
- Eyes
- Whiskers

These squares are very important for "cat".

2. Which squares are less important?

Tick the best answer:

□ Squares with background only

□ Squares with the cat's face

CAT OR NOT CAT?

Look at the important parts of each picture and decide.

Picture A

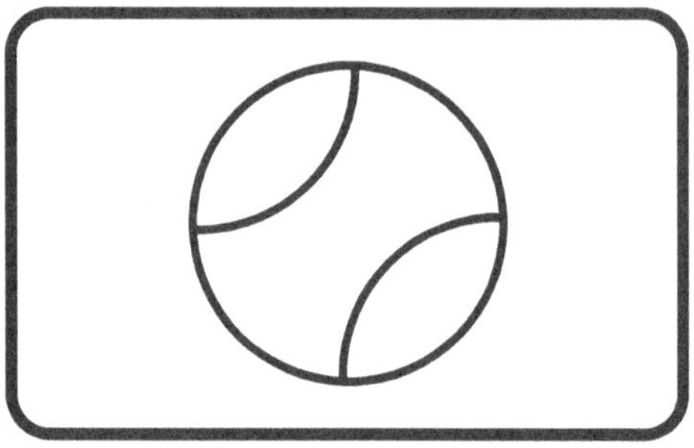

Picture B

1. Which picture is more likely "Cat"?

□ Picture A □ Picture B

2. Why did you choose that picture?

"Because it has ____."

(Hint: Think: ears? eyes? whiskers?)

3. Fill in the blanks:

"Deep learning looks at small parts of the picture and tries to find important __________."

4. Wise Owl's reminder:

Sometimes deep learning might still say "Cat" for something that is not a cat. Should humans check strange results?

□ Yes □ No

WHEN DEEP LEARNING IS WRONG

Even powerful AI can see things wrongly.
Wise Owl helps us check.

WISE OWL'S CHECK

1. For each picture, is the AI correct?

Write ✓ (right) or ✗ (wrong) in the box:

A. Toy cat → ______

B. Dog in cat costume → ______

C. Shadow on wall → ______

2. Fix one mistake.

Choose one picture where the AI was wrong and write what you think:

"For picture ____ the AI was wrong.

I think it is really a __________________."

3. Why must humans still check deep learning?

"Because sometimes the AI can be tricked by ______________________________."

(e.g., costumes, shadows, toys)

CHAPTER 3 CHECKPOINT – ML & DL EXPLORER

Time to Show what you remember about machine learning and deep learning.

Quick quiz

1. What is machine learning?
"Machine learning is when a computer learns from ________________________."
(Hint: data and examples)

2. What is a dataset?
□ A single picture
□ A big table of examples and labels
□ A type of test

3. What is a model?
"The model is the trained ________ that makes ________."

4. What is deep learning?
Tick the best sentence:
□ Using one big rule only
□ Using many tiny helpers in layers
□ A game about cats

You finished Chapter 3 – Great job, ML & DL Explorer!

Signed by: ______________________
(Parent / Guardian / Teacher)

This badge belongs to:

Chapter 4 – AI & ME (Smart & Safe Use)

AI AS A HELPER, NOT THE BOSS

AI can help us, but people should still make big decisions.

"AI helps with ideas and spelling."

"Doctors and parents decide about health."

THINK ABOUT AI AS A HELPER

1. In Scene A (homework):

AI can help with:

□ Spelling □ Ideas □ Doing all the homework alone

2. In Scene B (health):

Who should make the final decision?

□ Only the AI

□ Doctor and parents

3. Fill in the blanks:

"AI should be a ____________, not the ____________."

WHO SHOULD DECIDE?

For each situation, tick who should decide most of the time.

1. What video to watch next
□ Mostly AI (suggestions)
□ Mostly ME / ADULT

2. Whether an exam answer is correct
□ Mostly AI
□ Mostly TEACHER / ME

3. Who should be punished at school
□ Mostly AI
□ Mostly TEACHER / PRINCIPAL

4. How to spell a difficult word
□ Mostly AI
□ Mostly ME / ADULT

5. Which way to go in a busy city
□ Mostly MAP AI (like GPS)
□ Mostly HUMAN DRIVER

THINK & WRITE

1. One thing I am happy to let AI help with:

2. One thing humans should always decide:

3. One question I can ask before trusting AI:

"____?"

STAYING SAFE WITH AI

Wise Owl reminds us: Be kind. Be careful. Don't overshare.

"I will show strange answers to my parent / teacher."

WISE OWL'S SAFE AI RULES

1. Things that are OK to ask AI about:

□ School topics (math, science, history)
□ Story ideas and games
□ How to be better at a hobby

2. Things you should NOT type or tell AI:

□ Full name
□ Home address
□ Phone number
□ Passwords

3. If an answer feels strange or mean:

"Show it to a ____________ or ____________."
(Hint: parent, guardian, teacher)

SAFE OR NOT SAFE?

Tick SAFE or NOT SAFE for each AI chat message.

1. "Hi, can you explain gravity for my science homework?"
   □ SAFE □ NOT SAFE

2. "My name is Riya Sharma and I live at 12 Green Street."
   □ SAFE □ NOT SAFE

3. "Can you give me some ideas for a story about dragons?"
   □ SAFE □ NOT SAFE

4. "Here is my password so you can log in and help me."
   □ SAFE □ NOT SAFE

5. "Someone online was mean to me. What should I do?"
   □ SAFE □ NOT SAFE

6. "My phone number is 98_______. Call me!"
   □ SAFE □ NOT SAFE

WISE OWL'S QUESTIONS

1. If you ever feel upset or scared by something an AI says, who are two adults you can talk to?
2. Fill in the blanks:
"I will not share my full __________, __________, or __________with AI."
(Hint: name, address, phone number)

WISE OWL SAYS

"AI is a tool.
Your safety comes first."

IS THIS FAIR?

Sometimes AI can learn a rule that is not fair.
Wise Owl checks the rules.

Some kids wearing blue shirts look happy. Some kids wearing other colors (red, yellow) look confused/sad.

"If the rule is unfair, the AI can also be unfair."

WISE OWL'S FAIRNESS CHECK

The AI learned a rule:

"Only children wearing blue can join the game."

1. Is this a fair rule?

□ Yes □ No

2. Why or why not?

"I think this rule is ______________________________ because ____."

3. A better, fair rule could be:

"Anyone who ________________________________can join the game."

(Hint: Think of something fair, like "wants to play", "follows the rules", etc.)

FAIR OR UNFAIR?

Tick FAIR or UNFAIR for each rule.

1. "Everyone in the class can join the game if they finish their homework."
   □ FAIR □ UNFAIR
2. "Only children whose names start with A to M get extra marks."
   □ FAIR □ UNFAIR
3. "We listen to all students, not just the loudest ones."
   □ FAIR □ UNFAIR
4. "The AI only recommends books for tall students."
   □ FAIR □ UNFAIR
5. "If someone is new to school, we still give them a chance in the team."
   □ FAIR □ UNFAIR

THINK & WRITE

1. Why is it important for AI to be fair?
"If AI is unfair, some people ____."

2. How can humans help AI be fairer?
"Humans can check the rules and data and _______________________________."

3. One fair rule I like:
"A fair rule for my class or team is: ___________________________________."

"Humans must check the rules, not just trust AI."

AI IN MY DAY

Where does AI quietly help you from morning to night?

THINK ABOUT YOUR DAY

1. When do you think AI helps you?

Tick all that you use:

□ Music or video apps
□ Maps / directions
□ Online games
□ Homework or study apps
□ Online shopping or food apps

2. Circle two icons in the picture where you think AI is used.

(music, video, maps, robot helper, shopping)

3. Write one sentence:

"One helpful way AI is used in my day is: ______________________________."

4. And one time I should be more careful with AI:

"I should be extra careful when I use AI for: ____________________________."

MY AI PROMISES

Write or tick the promises you want to follow when you use AI.

PINKY PROMISE:

□ 1. I will not share my full name, address, phone number, or passwords with AI.
□ 2. I will use AI as a helper for ideas and understanding, not to cheat.
□ 3. If an AI answer looks mean, scary, or strange, I will show it to an adult.
□ 4. I will remember that AI can make mistakes, and I should still think for myself.
□ 5. I will be kind and polite when I write to AI.
□ 6. I will not use AI to hurt others or spread lies.

MY OWN PROMISES
Promise 1:

Promise 2:

Sign here:
(My name)

AI & ME: CHOOSING BETTER

Sometimes I can choose a better way to ask or use AI.

1. Homework help

A. "Write my whole answer for me so I don't have to think."

B. "Explain this topic in simple words so I can write my own answer."

Circle the better choice: A / B

2. Talking about a friend

A. "Tell me mean jokes about my friend."

B. "Give me ideas to solve a fight with my friend kindly."

Circle the better choice: A / B

3. Using AI late at night

A. "I will stay up all night chatting with AI instead of sleeping."

B. "I will stop using screens when it is my sleep time."

Circle the better choice: A / B

THINK & WRITE

"One good way I want to use AI is:

_______________________________________."

CHAPTER 4 CHECKPOINT – SMART AI USER

Show what you remember about using AI safely and wisely.

1. What is one thing you should NOT share with AI?

□ Your favourite color

□ Your full home address

□ Your favourite cartoon

2. If an AI answer feels mean or scary, what should you do?

"I should show it to a ___________ or ___________."

(Hint: parent, guardian, teacher)

3. AI is a...

□ Boss that decides everything

□ Helper that can still make mistakes

□ Magic that is always right

4. Tick the safe use of AI:

□ Asking AI to do all my exam answers

□ Asking AI to explain a topic so I understand it

□ Sharing my password so AI can "help"

You finished Chapter 4 – Great job, Smart AI User!

Signed by: ____________________

(Parent / Guardian / Teacher)

This badge belongs to:

GLOSSARY

AI BASICS

AI (Artificial Intelligence)
A computer program that can seem smart – it can learn, answer questions, and make decisions instead of only following one fixed rule.

Robot
A machine that can do actions in the real world, like moving, picking things up, or talking. Some robots use AI inside them.

AI Squad
The team of characters in this book:
Data Robot, Pattern Dragon, and Wise Owl.
They help you understand how AI works.

Pattern
Something that repeats in a clear way.
For example: red–blue–red–blue, or 2, 4, 6, 8.
AI and Pattern Dragon love finding patterns.

DATA & LEARNING

Data
The information we give to a computer or AI. It can be numbers, words, pictures, sounds, or videos.

Example
One piece of data with an answer.
For example: "Dog → animal" is one example.

Label
The correct answer for an example.
In "Dog → animal", the label is "animal".

Dataset

A big table or collection of many examples and their labels.
AI uses the dataset to learn.

Prediction

A guess made by the AI or model after learning.
Example: The model sees a picture and predicts “cat” or “not cat”.

MACHINE LEARNING & MODELS

Machine Learning (ML)

When a computer learns from data and examples instead of only following fixed rules written by humans.

Training

The study time for a model. The AI sees many examples with the correct answers and tries to learn a pattern.

Testing

The quiz time for a model. The AI sees new examples without answers and we check how well it does.

Model

The computer’s trained “brain” that is created after training. The model takes input and makes predictions.

Feedback

When humans correct the AI’s mistakes and give it the right answer, so it can learn and improve next time.

DEEP & SAFE AI

Deep Learning

A special kind of machine learning that uses many tiny helpers in layers to find complex patterns, like in pictures or voices.

Neural Network
The name for this layered system of tiny helpers.
It has an input layer, hidden layers, and an output layer.

Fairness
Being reasonable and equal to different people.
If the rule or data is unfair, the AI can also be unfair.

Privacy
Keeping your personal information safe.
This includes your full name, address, phone number, passwords, and private photos.

Safe AI Use
Using AI in a way that is kind, careful, and smart:
not oversharing, not cheating, and asking adults when something feels wrong.

"You can draft the glossary you'd like to have, and do it right here."

MATCH THE WORD

Draw a line from each word to its meaning.

AI

Data

Label

Dataset

Model

Training

Deep Learning

Fairness

A. A big table of many examples and their labels.

B. A computer program that can seem smart and make decisions.

C. The study time when the AI sees examples with answers.

D. The correct answer for one example, like “cat” or “not cat”.

E. A special kind of machine learning that uses many tiny helpers in layers.

F. Being reasonable and equal to different people, not picking favorites for silly reasons.

G. The computer’s trained “brain” that makes predictions.

H. The information we give to AI: numbers, words, pictures, etc.

AI WORD SEARCH

Find and circle these words in the grid:
AI, DATA, LABEL, MODEL, ROBOT, OWL, DRAGON, FAIR, SAFE

AI
DATA
LABEL
MODEL
ROBOT
OWL
DRAGON
FAIR
SAFE

```
S L N R S F E F K P V C
X Y T O G F U A O O V N
D U A Z A Z Q I A D E R
X A F S C E L R I G K O
N Y T S A W X E W Z E B
E Q M A Y G Z B D H B O
D R A G O N L F C O X T
X N L W T M S L A Y M K
L F V J Q Q A X A B Q L
D X Z O T B Y F E D U W
U M P B E Y D U H U G O
D Y D L Q F W J P R Q M
```

FILL IN THE BLANKS – WORD BANK

Use the word bank to fill the blanks.

Word Bank:

data **l**abels **d**ataset **m**odel **t**raining **d**eep learning **p**rivacy

Machine learning is when a computer learns from __________ and examples.

The correct answers for each example are called __________.

A big table of many examples and labels is a __________.

The computer's trained "brain" that makes predictions is the __________.

The study time when the AI sees examples with answers is called __________.

__________ is a special kind of machine learning that uses many tiny helpers in layers.

Keeping your personal information safe, like your address and phone number, is called __________.

UNSCRAMBLE THE AI WORDS

The letters are mixed up.
Unscramble them and write the correct AI word.

I A
→ ____________________
A T D A
→ ____________________
B A L E L
→ ____________________
D E O M L
→ ____________________
F A I R
→ ____________________
V I R A P Y
→ ____________________

BONUS:
Use two of the words above in a sentence:
"____
____."

DATA ROBOT MAZE

Help Data Robot reach the MODEL at the end of the maze

1. Use a pencil to find a path from START to MODEL.
2. On the way, think of one word you learned about AI.
   Write it here: ____________________________
3. Color Data Robot and the maze path.

AI SQUAD COMIC – PAGE 1

Create your own short comic about the
AI Squad helping someone.

Label near panel: Panel 1 – The Problem
"Draw and write what problem someone has.
(Maybe homework, a game, or a fairness issue.)"

Label near panel: Panel 2 – AI Squad Arrives
"Draw Data Robot, Pattern Dragon, and Wise Owl.
Show how they try to help."

Label near panel: Panel 3 – A Better Way
"Show a good and safe way they use AI to help.
Add speech bubbles if you like!"

You can continue your comic on the next page!

AI SQUAD COMIC – PAGE 2

Continue or start a new AI Squad adventure.

Title of my comic:

Draw your comic in these 4 panels.
Try to show:

- What happens next
- How the AI is used safely
- A happy or funny ending

“Great job, storyteller! – AI Squad”

THIS CERTIFIES THAT

____

(WRITE YOUR NAME)

HAS COMPLETED THIS BOOK AND LEARNED ABOUT AI, MACHINE LEARNING, DEEP LEARNING, SAFETY, AND FAIRNESS.

DATE: ________________

SIGNED (ADULT): ______________________________